D0746807

BUDDHISM

THROUGH CHRISTIAN EYES

ALEX G. SMITH

© OMF INTERNATIONAL
(formerly China Inland Mission)

Published by Overseas Missionary Fellowship (USA) Inc.
10 W. Dry Creek Circle, Littleton, CO 80120
Website: www.omf.org

Published 2001

ISBN 1-929122-10-1

Cover photo by Kevin Morris

OMF Books are distributed by
OMF, 10 West Dry Creek Circle, Littleton, CO 80120, USA
OMF, Station Approach, Borough Green, Sevenoaks, Kent TN15 8BG, United Kingdom
OMF, PO Box 849, Epping, NSW 2121, Australia
OMF, 5759 Coopers Ave., Mississauga, ON L4Z 1R9 Canada
OMF, PO Box 10159, Auckland, New Zealand
OMF, PO Box 3080, Pinegowrie 2123, South Africa
and other OMF offices

TABLE OF CONTENTS

INTRODUCTION

The recent growth and renewal of Buddhism, especially in the West, is a phenomenon of the last half century and is likely to increase into the 21st century. The interlacing of Buddhism and Christianity seems to be a growing fashion at the folk religion level.

The clouding of differences between Buddhism and Christianity can only be clarified as we clearly understand the principles and precepts foundational to both. So many think that these two great religious systems are quite similar. Actually they are extremely different at many points.

This book is needed today. It will help Christians and Buddhists alike understand each other better. Many Christians are largely ignorant of Buddhism and many Buddhists know little of fundamental Christian foundations. There are many varieties of both groups. This complicates simplicity of explanation.

Section 1 analyzes contemporary folk Buddhism, its growths and contrasts. Section 2 focuses on principles for effective communication in local cultures.

May this brief writing stir the hearts of both Christians and Buddhists to seek deeper truth with all their minds, souls and spirits. To that end I send this book forth.

March 30, 2001
Alex G. Smith, D.Miss.
Portland, Oregon U.S.A.

SECTION ONE

Recognizing Buddhism On The Move

Among the major world religions, Buddhism, with its emphasis on meditation, purity, peace and ethics, appears to be the most non-threatening. Contrast this image with the common perception of Islam with its frequent threats of terrorism, bombings and hijackings. The picture most Westerners have of Buddhism is that of the Dalai Lama — smiling, sophisticated, sweet and serene. Surprisingly in some "Christian" seminaries in the USA a large portrait of him has been placed prominently in their chapels, though photographs of Islamic leaders are never present.

A Burgeoning Billion

The phenomenal growth of Buddhism, particularly in the last quarter century, has made major inroads into the West. Historically Christianity was most popular in the West, and by the early 1900s the majority of Christians were still Westerners. But since then, major outreaches of missions have resulted in significant people movements, bringing multitudes on all continents into the Church. Consequently today the number of Christians located in the rest of the world is probably double that in the West.

Buddhism, on the other hand, was a major focus of the East, particularly in populous North, East and Southeast Asia. Significantly only in recent decades has it spread like wildfire throughout the West.

Today it claims ten million followers in the USA alone where over one thousand five hundred Buddhist temples are countable and hundreds of Buddhist associations flourish. No wonder the notable historian Arnold Toynbee wrote that the latter half of the 20th century would be marked by "the interpenetration of Buddhism and Christianity." According to *Christianity Today* (Dec. 6, 1999, p.34) University of Chicago sociologist Stephen R. Warner told Religion News Service, "The world of American religion is going through enormous change. It will be increasingly difficult to distinguish Christians and Buddhists."

Today Buddhism strongly influences about a billion people, many of whom would be classified as "folk Buddhists." An estimated figure popularly quoted for Roman Catholics today is one billion. Protestants also claim one billion. Like the folk Buddhist billion, these are largely nominal "folk Christians."

A Syncretistic Mix

The impact from the spread of Buddhism may be illustrated by a product from a kitchen blender. Blend bananas—representing animism or Shintoism, apples—depicting indigenous religions like Taoism and Confucianism, and throw in pears—indicative of tribal belief structures. The composite mixture in the blender still remains a light, creamy color. Then add strawberries—symbolizing Buddhism, and the whole mixture is changed suddenly, saturated with a pink hue. That is precisely the effect of Buddhism. It eclectically absorbed but did not alienate indigenous religions or animism. Under its Doctrine of Assimilation, Buddhism dominated but did not dislodge these elements. In fact, in his excellent studies among Buddhist peoples, Dr. S.J. Tambiah of Cambridge University claims that while Westerners may analyze Buddhism into different religious elements — Buddhistic, animistic, Brahmanistic, Taoistic and others, the folk Buddhist sees those elements as one integrated whole, namely Buddhism. Like the mix in the blender, Buddhism permeates the whole and blends all together without losing the flavor of each element. Thus we find many variegated varieties of folk Buddhism throughout the world.

Major Schools and Cults
The plethora of Buddhist "denominations" with their innumerable cults is quite astounding. Here Buddhism certainly shows its tolerance, without sacrificing its basic integrative doctrinal foundations. Buddhism has many faces throughout the world. Primarily, however, there are two major schools: the conservative Theravada, known as Southern Buddhism, and the liberal Mahayana, known as Northern and Eastern Buddhism. Theravada tends to be focused mostly in Sri Lanka and Southeast Asia, though even there elements of Mahayana are commonly mixed in as well. Mahayana covers the globe, with major concentrations in East Asia. The Kwan Yin Buddhist cult, emphasizing a female bodhisattva of mercy, has revived and expanded worldwide, particularly in the latter 1900s. Truly there is little pure Buddhism on earth, except among some dedicated intellectual Buddhists and long-term committed priests.

Nevertheless, Buddhism is the integrating and identifying religion of approximately one billion. Buddhism is bigger than you think. Theravada accounts for about 150 million people. Mahayana accounts for approximately 850 million folk Buddhists, including around 16 million followers of Tantric Tibetan Buddhism, also known as Lamaism, Vajrayana, or Mantrayana. Tibetan Buddhism acknowledges the Dalai Lama as its visible head. It is quite popular in the USA because of the presence, policies and political cause of the Dalai Lama. Major branches of the Mahayana school include Tendai, Zen, Pure Land, Nichiren, Soka Gakkai and many others. Japan particularly has a proliferation of Buddhist cults. Probably 70% of the Japanese adhere to some form of Buddhism. In China on July 22, 1999, the PRC authorities outlawed the Falun Gong cult, which incorporates Tai Chi with Buddhist meditation and practices. Popular even among Communists government officials, this Buddhist cult claims over 160 million adherents. Currently Falun Gong is administered and run out of New York via the Internet.

Beliefs and Behaviors
The basic beliefs of Buddhism are well known. Meditating on the Middle Way, Siddharta Gautama intuitively realized the Four Noble Truths which focus on the condition, cause and cure of universal suffering. The Buddha taught that by following the Eight-fold Path of self-effort one could escape life's suffering, and its changing illusion. Attaining enlightenment by eliminating all desires (the cause of suffering), one enters Nirvana which primarily is a state of escape (a breaking free from the endless cycles of birth and rebirth).

Underneath and behind Buddhist beliefs are strong concepts of karma and reincarnation, borrowed or adapted from Hinduism, out of which it was a reactionary renewal movement. From the start the Buddha rejected all gods and spiritual beings, including the concept of humans as living souls. He considered everything to be changing, illusionary and impermanent. Only by self deliverance and doing good can one hope to proceed to a better reincarnation and eventually, after tens of thousands of births and rebirths, hopefully attain Nirvana.

Such kinds of ideal beliefs are common in many religions, but the "real" behavior of their followers is often quite different. Many follow basic Buddhist precepts, but the majority also practice many of the elements rejected by the Buddha, including belief in gods, spirits, ancestor worship, and many other indigenous forms of religion. Thus a multitude of forms of Buddhism have been proliferated. This population of a billion people is a crucial challenge for the Church of the 21st century. Buddhist peoples are the neglected giant in mission. Even among the Christian community, many are unknowingly affected by subtle Buddhist ideas. Recently someone introduced herself to a relative of mine as a "Jesus Buddhist." Last year a friend received a Christmas card from a Christian associate signed "In Zen." Among Christians and occasionally from pulpits one hears Buddhist connotations commonly being spoken today such as "nirvana," "in a former life," "it's my karma," "my next reincarnation," "let your mind go blank," "dig deep down within you," and so on. This is a subtle effect of the "blender" of Buddhism.

Trouble in "Paradise"
Lately some cracks and crevices have appeared in Buddhism, though divisions and controversies are not new to this religion. The *Bangkok Post* of February 19, 1999, reported that, according to Phra Dhammapitaka, a highly respected Thai monk, aberrant schisms had arisen at Wat Dhammakaya. These were "corrupting the doctrine and discipline of Theravada Buddhism" and "negates Buddha." Such teachings and practices were contrary to the basic tenets of the Dhamma and the Sangha (Order of the Monks). Those who propagated divergent doctrines such as "Nirvana is a permanent heaven thus possessing *atta*, or self," were promptly disciplined and proscribed. Other charges included "commercialization of Buddhism, monks' misconduct and opaque business investments."

Incidents of priests being defrocked for moral lapses or corruption are not uncommon. During the summer of 1999 in Japan, the Nichiren Shoshu High Priest ordered the destruction of the expensive and ornate

Shohondo, the Grand Worship Hall at the foot of sacred Mt. Fuji. The festering cause was sparked by longtime internal conflicts and power struggles among the thirty Nichiren sects, especially with reference to the Soka Gakkai. Around 150,000 members left Shoshu. Bitter rivalries also still exist among sects in Tibetan and other groups. The Aum Shinrikyo (Supreme Truth) was a doomsday Buddhist cult in Japan that went awry when its leader, Shoko Asahara, began to call himself a Messiah. The result of their misinterpreting Buddhism sadly ended, according to *Newsweek* June 1, 1998, with the 1995 lethal attack on the Tokyo subway system, "releasing deadly sarin gas that killed a dozen people and made 5,000 others sick." Despite these aberrant examples, Buddhism is on the move and growing.

Resurgence and Resistance
The First International Buddhist Propagation Conference was held in Kyoto, Japan April 8-13, 1998. A key discussion centered around the growing concern to protect existing Buddhist populations from religious change. Prominent Buddhist leaders from 17 Asian countries attended, although the notable absence of key representatives of Shinshu and Zen Buddhist sects in Japan was striking. Strong statements against those groups' "proselytizing" Buddhists were made. The Venerable Dr. K. Sri Dhammananda, a leading Buddhist scholar and prolific author from Sri Lanka noted that "poverty and ignorance were exploited to convert inno-cent Buddhists and to disrupt their ancient cultures and practices. Many countries which were buddhist (sic) are in danger of losing their buddhist predominance due to these despicable methods employed by these so called 'evangelists'."

In most Southeast Asian countries restrictions on spreading the gospel are already legally in place, although not always strongly enforced. In Laos pressure is put on all Christians to attend anti-religion seminars propagating the government and party line. Encouraged by the Buddhist majority in a Communist-ruled situation, officials demand each person to sign documents before the authorities, affirming that they will resign from all foreign religions, involvement in which is interpreted as being illegal activity. Their signatures enjoin the government and Party to punish them appropriately for any infractions thereof. A similar movement is afoot in Vietnam, particularly targeting Hmong Christians. *Maranatha Christian Journal*, October 1, 1999, reports that radical Buddhists in Myanmar (Burma) have declared Christian radio broadcasting a threat to Buddhism, and have specifically named some Christian agencies as culpable. The extremists with other Buddhist leaders have distributed documents listing systematic methods for eliminating Christianity.

Aggressive Buddhist outreach is also increasing, particularly in the West. A former Nichiren member says that the largest Buddhist temple in the USA, located in Hacienda Heights, California, was built primarily as a Buddhist missionary training center to reach Westerners. *Los Angeles Times*, dated October 2, 1999, describes the new private Soka Buddhist University currently being constructed by Soka Gakkai International in Aliso Viejo, California. Twelve of the seventeen administrators are SGI members. Early in the year 2000 Buddhist monks officially dedicated "Thai Town" in the Hollywood area of Los Angeles. About 70,000 Buddhist Thai live nearby. In Northern Thailand outreaches to tribal groups by the Buddhists resulted in whole villages of Karen and other tribes becoming Buddhist, including some former Christian villages. Buddhism is on the move.

IDENTIFYING CURRENT TRENDS AND CONCERNS

Renewed Contextualization

With the Dalai Lama's example and encouragement, and in order to make Buddhism more palatable to North Americans, Tibetan Buddhists have endeavored to reduce the magic and Tantric elements, except for the *sand mandalas* which invoke the spirits and deities to be present and resident. Mandalas have already been set up in some Canadian and American cities, including Los Angeles and Chicago. The Dalai Lama's 1996 book on Jesus, *The Good Heart: Buddhist Perspectives on the Teachings of Jesus* published by Wisdom, has attracted some Christians to Buddhism. His popular writings emphasize the new foci of Buddhism: ethics for the new millennium, happiness, liberation, tolerance and "peace without religion."

Also played down is the fact that fundamental Buddhism relegates to women an inferior position. In Theravada Buddhism, until a woman is reborn as a man she has no hope of ever attaining *Nirvana*. This scaled back low key approach has influenced many unsuspecting Americans, especially as Hollywood films have publicly popularized Buddhist tenets and philosophies. Key well-liked actors, talk-show hosts, and even some high level politicians openly identify themselves with Buddhism. The January 2000 issue of *Civilization* magazine claimed a "Buddha boom" was progressing in the West. This described how big business and economics have been tied in, so that "Boardroom Buddhism" is now commonplace.

New Buddhist approaches and outreach have also been contextualized by adopting Christian evangelistic methods and strategies. For example, in Korea the traditional Buddhist temples were isolated up in the mountains away from the population concentrations. Today, however, many Korean priests have moved down into the cities and urban centers to set up "house temples." This occurs also in the USA. Converts to Soka Gakkai have long used "the cell group" approach, like churches do. In various Buddhist lands, in order to become more compatible with Christian response, some Buddhists adapt Christian forms of singing and music in their services, preach in the vernacular language, and add Sunday schools to their programs. In Myanmar some Buddhist priests even use the Bible selectively to preach and interpret their doctrines. In the West some Protestant church buildings have been converted into Buddhist temples.

Practical Issues
This new explosion of the Buddhist world should awaken urgent responses from theologians and missiologists. First, it demands a critique of current Christianity so as to acknowledge our failures and to repent of our weaknesses. It calls for concerted efforts

towards the renewal of the church. Second, it requires a careful evaluation of the Christian ministry, especially service to those outside the church. A redeployment of people and resources to catalyze an accelerated transformation of society is needed. New efforts to stimulate fresh energies in evangelism, practical social concern and cross-cultural mission must become the driving force and vision for the church in the world of the 21st century. A new wave of compassion, consideration and love for fellow humans will sensitize the church to the needs and opportunities that abound in all communities. Buddhist neighbors and peoples around the globe are to be full recipients of God's love and His gospel also. This task is not easy. Third, it calls for some to develop a deeper analytical understanding of folk Buddhism and to comprehend the ramifications for the church's role and contribution in serving within Buddhist influenced societies. Here considerable research and experimentation are required.

Theological Concerns
While there may seem to be some congruency between Christianity and Buddhism, the contradictions are glaring and significant. Certainly the Buddhists model examples for the church in maintaining discipline within the clergy and in defending high standards of purity in their fundamental teachings. They discern deviant and divergent doctrine and discipline those who exceed acceptable limits. The church should continue to do this also. However, the underemphasized gift of discernment is probably more crucial for this time than ever before. Relativism, humanism, universalism and many other "isms" assail the Christian doctrine and message. Theological and missiological discerners are needed today. Vital distinctions and differentiations between Buddhism and Christianity call for clarification

in order to avoid confusion and to sharpen clouded conceptualizations.

Some theological issues contrasting these two religions which need clear differentiation and exposition include: 1) divine revelation or human intuition, 2) the nature of God—personal Creator/controller or impersonal non-being (like karma), 3) the nature of Christ—God/man or only human, redeeming substitute or impotent to help, 4) the nature of life—one single life or a circle of multiple lives via reincarnation, 5) sin—transgression or illusion, 6) the means of salvation—faith or works, grace or karmic merit, divine provision or self effort. Many other similar differences show that these two religious perspectives are truly diametrically opposed. Many suggested similarities are mostly superficial.

Furthermore, meaning discrepancy is a serious semantic problem in discussions between Buddhists and Christians. The use of similar words does not mean equivalent meanings in both religions. Even the same symbols may have very divergent definitions and connotations. For example some Buddhist scholars like Bhikku Buddhadasa Indapanno say Buddhists believe in God. In The Sinclaire Thompson Memorial Lectures: *Christianity and Buddhism* printed in 1967, he interpreted God to be equivalent to karma (cause and effect) and also to ignorance (a source of suffering). For those engaged in dialogue or debate, careful identification of discrepancy in meaning will be crucial to full understanding. Not being on the same page guarantees failure to reach agreement or to arrive at adequate conclusions.

Missiological Challenges
With specific reference to folk Buddhists, missiological issues to be studied are numerous. I suggest three significant questions: 1) Can the Buddhist concept of

transfer of merit from priests or bodhisattvas and other sources be compared with Christ's grace through His substitutionary sacrifice? Does human effort and merit equate with God's propitiation through Christ? 2) Can the concept of a future Maitreya Buddha be used as a redemptive analogy fulfilled in Jesus Christ, or only as a point of contact from which to proceed towards the gospel? Does such a redemptive analogy give too high a credence of revelation to Buddhist scriptures? Is being a "Messianic Buddhist" acceptable to either the church or to the Sangha? Buddhist scholars would deny such a possibility because this is still the Age of Gautama Buddha, so Christ's coming around 2000 years ago already negates the possibility that He fulfilled the coming Buddha. 3) Can the church and missions maintain contextual credibility with the current threat of new syncretism in the church at home and abroad? What dangers lie ahead because of confusing definitions and the clouding of distinctions between Christian and Buddhist perspectives and principles? What must be done to preserve the faith and foundations of Christianity in today's pluralistic climate? It seems that rough rapids of opposition and persecution will increasingly face the church in the future. If she is to maintain her mandate to make disciples of all peoples, tongues, tribes and nations, a new genuineness in loving service and a heightened sensitivity in witness to the Savior will be required.

Chapters 1 and 2 were originally printed in the
Occasional Bulletin of the Evangelical Missiological Society
Vol. 13 No. 2, Spring 2000

FINDING AND DEFINING
THE BUDDHIST WORLD

The prophet Daniel was in a Babylonian palace when a Hindu prince, Gautama Siddharta, was born in a palace of the Shakya tribe in northern India (now Nepal). This was about 560 years before Jesus Christ was born. Israel was already in captivity, under God's judgment for failing as God's people. The glorious Temple had been destroyed 23 years earlier. Gautama became the founder of Buddhism. About that time, the rise of other Eastern religions occurred, including

Confucianism, Taoism, Shintoism, and Jainism. It seems Israel's spiritual demise opened the door for a wave of new humanistic religions. What a lesson for the church in today's pluralistic times!

Three periods

The life of Gautama is seen in three periods. First was affluence. His father pampered him with luxury and pleasure, protecting him from seeing pain and suffering, and preventing him from contact with death and decay. By nineteen, he was married and had a son.

Then the second period started when, one day he went beyond the protective walls of the palace and saw the sights of four people—old, sick, dead, and an ascetic. This shocked him, and that night, without waking his wife or son, he left the palace. For the next six years, he followed the rigorous austerity of an ascetic, disciplined life. One day, because of weakness from fasting, he almost drowned while bathing. He realized that this stringent path did not provide the answers to life.

He returned to Bodh Gaya where he started on the third period of seeking and inquiring. He deeply meditated under the Bo fig tree for seven weeks. During this time he received enlightenment, including the Four Noble Truths: 1) All is suffering. 2) The cause of suffering is desire. 3) The solution is to extinguish desire. 4) The method to do so is through the Eight-fold Path.

Denying the existence of God, soul or spiritual beings, the Buddha, as he was now called, taught that Karma (cause and effect) of past lives resulted in the constant circle of birth, death, and rebirth (reincarnation). He believed the only way to be free of this is through individual self-effort. Immediately he found five ascetic men and preached to them in Deer Park. They were converted and formed the first Buddhist Sangha or community. He also saw many family members and famous people become his followers. The Buddha died about 480 BC, probably of food poisoning.

Expansion
For the next two hundred years, Buddhism was confined to north India. Then it expanded dramatically under King Asoka (274 - 232 BC). He consolidated his conquests by sending out Buddhist missionaries to preach and convert the people—north, south, east, and west. Thus, all of India came under Buddhist sway. Asoka also sent his own relative as a missionary to Ceylon. Buddhism spread into China, Afghanistan, and as far away as Greece and Cyrene (North Africa). Later it expanded through Korea and Japan, the East Indies (Indonesia), and throughout Southeast Asia. Within 1,500 years, Buddhism had covered and largely controlled the cultures of Asia. It has maintained a dominant influence in Asia ever since.

From the early Nestorians' outreach to Ceylon (537 AD) and to China (635 AD), Christian missions faced strong resistance from Buddhist peoples. Minimal fruit for Christianity occurred, usually under one percent, except in South Korea, though over two-thirds of that country still does not acknowledge Christ. Christian outreach in Buddhist lands is like slicing a sword through a lake's water. Immediately thereafter no perceptible impression is seen.

Assimilation
In contrast, wherever Buddhism spread, it had a vacuum cleaner effect, sucking up indigenous religions under its broad umbrella. Thus, it dominated and integrated local belief structures including animism and other isms, but did not dislodge nor destroy them. Therefore, a great variety of Buddhist societies arose. The amalgamation of many religious elements under

Buddhism produced a strong national, racial, and religious identity with Buddhism. This has become the strongest barrier to conversion and an obstinate obstacle to evangelization. "To be Thai, Burmese, Tibetan, Lao . . . is to be Buddhist." The strength of this underlying philosophy and conceptualization among the Asian peoples was seen when the repressive, stringent pressure of Communism was released in the early 1990s. Buddhism immediately bounced back in countries such as Mongolia, Vietnam and China, just like a rubber ball is restored immediately the pressure of the thumb is released.

A Global Religion

Today, in its variegated forms, the all-pervasive influence of a Buddhist world view saturates Asian peoples and envelopes all continents, including the 20th century popular inroads into the West. It did decline in India when it was reabsorbed by Hinduism, though a new revival movement recently arose there. Buddhism today influences about one billion people, primarily ranging from south Russia to Indonesia, and from west India to Japan. Significantly, this is the eastern half of the 10/40 Window where almost one half of humanity lives and where the majority of unreached peoples are found. Most of them are affected by some form of Buddhism. Thus, the challenge to the church of the 21st century is to sacrifice through patience, perseverance, and purity of life in order to reach this large remaining Buddhist bloc. Here is a call to pray, to go, to send, to evangelize, and to plant churches among all Buddhist peoples of Asia. OMF has worked among Buddhists for the last 135 years. Join us and others in advancing the gospel to them in the 21st century.

First published in East Asia's Millions Spring 1999

COMMUNICATING WITH
THE BUDDHIST MIND

The shadow of the Bo tree, originally casting its canopy over Nepal only, has spread in the last 2,500 years. Today Buddhism holds vast influence over much of Asia, particularly the East and the Southeast. Its broad shade also now extends to all continents. In its many variegated forms Folk Buddhism holds sway over one billion of the earth's inhabitants.

Like an invisible vapor, it has enveloped the globe, even infiltrating the thinking of unsuspecting Christians. Its dramatic quiet growth arose through traveling business people, Asian immigrants and refugees, direct missionary efforts, and its all-pervasive eclectic absorption of and penetration into other belief structures including New Age. As a result, today this mixing of Buddhism and Christianity is prevalent.

In this age of pluralistic thinking, many believe that one doesn't need to worry about the clouding of theological definitions or the reducing of the biblical mandate "to make disciples of all the ethnic peoples." After all, they say, all religions believe in God and are parallel ways to reach out to the Creator.

Having been an OMF missionary to Thailand for almost 20 years, I have often heard the Buddhist Thai respond to Christ's gospel: "Oh, Buddhism and Christianity are just the same." While some superficial similarities seem to exist between Buddhism and Christianity, there are some significant and serious differences. Following are some core Buddhist beliefs which I will compare with the beliefs of Christianity.

There is No God

The biblical concept of a supreme personal God who exists outside of His creation and who, in power and glory, brought all things into being is denied by Buddhism. All supernatural beings, including angels, demons and all gods were rejected by the Buddha. One well-known Buddhist pundit wrote that he believed in God, but then explained that God must be equated with either "ignorance" or karma! Thai students often said that if I could show them God then they would believe in Jesus. I simply asked them to show me first the scent of a rose or describe what the essence of electricity looks like. Neither are visible but nonetheless exist and can be experienced.

Christ's Deity Denied
As the perfect God-man, Christ is the only sinless Savior of the world. Often I have asked my Buddhist audience whom they thought Jesus was. Replies included: a good man, a prophet, the founder of the Christian religion, and the younger brother of the Buddha! The concept of Christ's deity is incomprehensible to the Buddhist mind.

Man is Not a Spiritual Being
The Bible teaches that man and woman were "made in the image of God." All are spiritual beings possessing a precious eternal quality. Humans are living souls with personality, value and dignity. The Buddha did not hold to mankind having soul or personality. To him, people were impermanent and transitory, ever facing the problem of how to escape from suffering. All life is meaningless. Christ received, however, brings rich fulfillment and gives true meaning to life.

Karma is the Iron Law
In Buddhism karma is the iron law. No one escapes either reincarnation or suffering. This engenders fatalistic attitudes. In contrast, Christ's gospel offers hope,

salvation and optimism for both present and future, even in the midst of suffering. I remember working with Mr. Yu, a leprosy patient in Thailand. As a Buddhist he believed that in previous incarnations he must have been extremely bad to have contracted such a dreadful disease. Because he lost toes and fingers and even much of his nose to leprosy, he had given up on life and just wanted to die. Then OMF missionaries contacted, treated and witnessed to Mr. Yu. He later accepted Christ, was rehabilitated, trained in Bible and given a livelihood. He served as a fruitful evangelist and an energetic pastor for about three decades. The power of Christ brought positive changes to his life.

Sin Has No Consequences
The two systems' concepts of sin stand in stark contrast. To Buddhists sin does not have any consequences before a holy God. It is not defined by doctrine, for to them existence is sin. They think that "desire" or transitory deception is sin. Popularly, sin is killing life in any form. Sin is believed to be the effect of one's karma. I remember a Thai woman once saying to me, "I have never sinned." It is difficult to help one who does not sense a need. At best, sin is an illusion, though the karmic consequences will accumulate for those who fail to break the endless cycles of reincarnation. The Christian identifies sin as a principle in all humankind, a flaw resulting from the Fall. In practice, sins are violations of God's character, an affront to Him by missing the mark, and subsequently moral failures.

Salvation Through Self
To the Christian, salvation is possible only through the grace of God in the provision of Christ. In Buddhism, no savior exists. In fact, the Buddha said he could not help anyone; he could only point the way. Each must

deliver one's self. Thus, by humanism Folk Buddhists attempt self deliverance by doing massive good works and making merit. One must overcome karma by self effort. The concept of substitution is lacking in Buddhism. It is difficult to comprehend and accept Christ's substitutionary death. This poses a major problem in the evangelization of Buddhist peoples. Fortunately, I found an illustration from Thai folklore that portrays substitution. Long ago, a king from the South besieged the king of Chiangmai in the North. Rather than see the city destroyed, the two kings agreed to select one man each for a contest to see who could stay under water the longest. The two men dived into the river. The first to emerge was the man from the South. Freedom for Chiangmai was assured. When the North's man did not come up, the king sent men in to search for him. They found he had tied himself to a tree limb and so deliberately sacrificed his life for the city.

Death, Not Life
There are other contrasts between these two religions, such as impermanence and eternity, self-centered orientation and altruism, but the most glaring contrast is that the ultimate "hope" in Buddhism is death or extinction. In Christ it is eternal life.

Biblical Truth and Outreach
These belief systems are not similar but rather diametrically opposed. This challenges churches today in two ways: to shore up the foundations of biblical truth with true knowledge and discernment; and to renew urgent outreach to the billion Buddhists in concerted prayer and by loving and meaningful ministry. Let Christians help banish ignorance by sharing the gospel of Christ, the living Redeemer, with all.

First published in East Asia's Millions, Spring 1999

Praying For Buddhist Peoples

Buddhism is alive and well in the 21st century. At the same time Christianity in the West seems to be lacking in fervor and commitment. Probably the best exercise for Christians to practice in modern times is to commit to concerted prayer for our world today. Consecrated intercession for the Buddhist World and other unreached peoples demands much discipline and determination. Dedication to meditating on God's Word and translating that into supplication to the Lord is vital for our generation.

The Burden

An American professional couple who are my encouraging friends have for years prayed for missionaries and motivated their church to get involved in spreading the gospel. Normally they go to Europe for vacation in midyear. For the summer of 2000 they decided to change and go to Thailand instead. This literally transformed them. They reported that "it was an eye-opening experience." They loved the Thai people, but were shocked by the prevailing Buddhism and its enormous power over the populace. They saw temples galore, idols without number, abundant devotees, and no lack of saffron-robed priests. On their return they wrote, "Our burden for the lost caught into Buddhism has grown exponentially. We have been intensely praying for the Buddhist World." Now that's a burden!

Tough Work

In lands where Buddhism prevails, the gospel languishes in its impact. Preaching the gospel there is like trying to hold back an avalanche. Generally today the church among Buddhist nations such as Japan,

Thailand, Myanmar, Mongolia, and other Buddhistic peoples elsewhere is really tiny, usually less than 1%. Evangelizing in the Buddhist World is like repeatedly banging one's head against a proverbial brick wall, making no perceptible impact.

Tribal groups in Buddhist lands have been much more receptive to the gospel than the Buddhist people themselves. In Myanmar and Thailand, 97% of the Christians there are tribal, though these ethnic peoples are in the minority. Recalculating Christian percentages from among Buddhist peoples without the Christianized tribes reveals a desperate need and a shockingly low proportion of Christians from among the Buddhist groups. But in recent years some encouraging signs of church growth have been occurring in pockets around the world. God is at work even in the Buddhist World! A burden to pray for these peoples is not only a significant, but also a strategic challenge. Tears of intercession with a deep love and concern for Folk Buddhists worldwide will move the church forward on its knees. OMF is encouraging the launching of a new movement of prayer calling for "*A Million Praying for a Billion Buddhists.*" We need to pray consistently as part of a team with this burden. Andrew Murray said, "He who prays most helps most." Will you join us in praying for the Buddhist World?

Praying Biblically
1. Praise the Lord of the Church that "a people for His Name" will be established among every unreached Buddhist nation, tribe, people and tongue. (Rev. 7:9-10)
2. Bind the forces of darkness, resisting all demonic rulers and spiritual powers which, in heavenly places, influence Buddhist countries among others. (Eph. 6:12-13, Dan. 10:13, 20)

3. Break down spiritual strongholds and human philosophies or arguments against God which produce barriers of resistance through social solidarity among Buddhists. (2 Cor. 10:4-5)
4. Claim Christ's complete victory over all demonic hordes that blind and enslave almost one billion Buddhists, including Han Chinese. (Col. 2:15)
5. Pray out "God-sent, willing, skillful workers" for each of many hundreds of unreached Buddhist people groups. (Matt. 9:38)
6. Intercede for lasting fruit from the sacrifice of existing missionaries of the various agencies working among Buddhists. (John 12:24)
7. Plead with our Lord for the opening of Buddhists' eyes to the revelation of the true and living God and His Christ, the unique Savior. (Eph. 1:17-23)
8. Believe God to enlighten the minds of Buddhists about the folly of making images and practicing idolatry. (Psa. 115:4-8)
9. Ask God to help Christians discern the biblical differences between Buddhist terms and the gospel so they can intelligently communicate the gospel. (Prov. 2:2-3; 2 Tim. 2:7)
10. Pray for Buddhist hearts to understand the gospel, especially the doctrines of Christ's substitution and redemption. (Gal. 3:13; 1 Pet. 1:18-29, 2:24)
11. Intercede for Buddhists and their families to come to faith in Christ, repenting from their total dependence on their own good works. (Eph. 2:8-9)
12. Pray for protection and nurture of new believers from Buddhist cultures, claiming God's protective "wall of fire around them." (Zech. 2:5; Psa. 91)
13. Ask that believers will share the gospel as bold witnesses to their Buddhist families, friends and neighbors. (Acts 4:29-31)
14. Uphold all Christians in Buddhist lands before the

Throne of God that they will exhibit holy, disciplined lifestyles as examples and models of Christ. (2 Cor. 3:2-3; 1 Pet. 1:15-16; 2:21)

15. Plead with God to multiply churches and begin church-planting movements among each Buddhist people group. (Matt. 16:18; 1 Pet. 2:9-10)

16. Intercede for the raising up of national church leaders to train and care for God's flocks and to extend the church into each Buddhist group. (Acts 20:27-32; 1 Pet. 5:1-4)

Helpful Resources

Resources for stimulating information and materials of Christian concern for Buddhists include:

1) *Days of Enlightenment: Prayer for Buddhists*, a pocket-sized 15-day selected prayer guide available from International Mission Board Resource Center, Richmond VA (e-mail: resource.center@imb.org).

2) *One Billion Wait* materials such as videos, pamphlets and books from OMF International, 10 West Dry Creek Circle, Littleton CO 80120-4413.

3) *Tearing Down Strongholds: Prayer for Buddhists*, by Elizabeth Wagner, Living Books for All, PO Box 98425 (TST) Kowloon, Hong Kong.

4) *Siamese Gold: The Church in Thailand*, by Alex G. Smith, Kanok Bannasan (OMF Publishers) Dindaeng, Bangkok, Thailand.

5) Website: www.us.omf.org or direct www.onebillionwait.org.

*"Praying Biblically" was first published in
East Asia's Millions, Spring 1999*

Sharing Life With Buddhists

In today's pluralistic climate it is important to learn how to live and share with others of differing viewpoints. To do so without sacrificing personal convictions or compromising Christian standards takes much tact, charity and understanding. This especially relates to sharing our Christian witness with Buddhist neighbors and friends. I suggest three practical actions for consideration.

Clarify Essential Concepts

Between Christians and Buddhists there exists much misunderstanding about the definition and meanings of the terms and concepts, falsely taken as equivalent to each other. Patient discussion may help clarify these foundational beliefs.

Christians must clearly explain key concepts that are most difficult for Buddhists to comprehend or accept. The use of analogy, stories, and illustration as skylights for understanding should be used along with relevant Scripture. Here are some topics:

1. Creation and the nature of the universe. Concrete reality versus transitory illusion needing detachment.
2. God, transcendent and personal as Creator and Controller versus over all impersonal void or nothingness.
3. Christ's deity and uniqueness as the God/man and sacrificial Redeemer versus only a human Jesus.
4. Nature of humankind with soul/spirit versus karmic recycling lacking soul/spirit.
5. Nature of sin as rebellious nature and selfish acts affronting a holy God versus an illusion, "ignorance" or killing life.

6. Grace freely bestowed through Christ versus the absolute law of karma.
7. Salvation through Christ's substitutionary death in our place versus unrelenting karma.
8. Regeneration through new birth versus reincarnation of accumulated karmic consequences.
9. Destiny in eternal resurrection life versus virtual extinction (release of existence) of nirvana.

Have Confidence

1. Be sure God is working sovereignly in the lives of those He is calling into His Church. So trust God to do His work.
2. Be aware that the Holy Spirit is the primary agent of mission in producing conviction and conversion. Only God's Spirit can open blind eyes to see the truth of Christ. So find out where God is working and get alongside.
3. Only the powerful Word of God proclaimed, clearly understood, and received by faith can transform lives, families, societies and whole people groups dominated by Buddhist influence and secular humanism anywhere. So meditate on, memorize and share God's Word sensitively and appropriately.
4. Be faithful in following Christ's model: Jesus "went about doing good" (Acts 10:38). Only the godly living witness of Christ in Christians, national believers and missionaries can demonstrate God's love and peace to Buddhists. So be "living letters about Christ."
5. Be available as God's instruments of service. Jonathan Bonk says, "Jesus' life was filled with divine interruptions." These were opportunities to proclaim, to serve, and to heal, even at most inconvenient times. So be ready and prepared to minister always.

6. Be hopeful, for Jeremiah said, "Ye shall seek me and ye shall find me when you shall search for me with all your heart" (Jer. 29:13). So be expectant and positive.
7. Be dependent always on Christ through prayer, obedience, and faith. So intercede faithfully.

Practice Love and Patience

1. Remember to pray first! Ask God to open minds, hearts and eyes spiritually. Request the Lord to give discernment and wisdom, and to bring every thought captive through obedience to Christ.
2. Respect the followers of other faiths as human beings whom God created with dignity. Do not destroy their faith, but help transfer their faith from the wrong object to the right one.
3. Reflect models of the Christian home with moral and ethical living yourself.
4. Rigorously earn the right to speak—be credible, honest, and loving with integrity and humility.
5. Recognize that all religions have some good in them.
6. Reject any attitude to judge, criticize, or make fun of others' beliefs. Open up discussion and dialogue with them on why they believe as they do.
7. Relate to them in true Christian love and genuine affection. Be good neighbors—truly friendly and genuinely caring.
8. Be ready to share Christ. Give them God's Word as appropriate occasion or interest arises.
9. Resist the temptation to pressure them to believe or to listen to the gospel. Only the Spirit persuades. Serve them sensitively and patiently as opportunity affords. For example, pray for them when they are sick, encourage them in trouble, help them in crisis.

10. Rejoice at what God is doing and will do in their lives and families.

Illustrating These Practices

The following true story elucidates these fundamental principles. The names of the two men have been changed to protect them. Some years ago I met Mr. Tawd, an elderly gentleman who was a Buddhist priest for 20 years before he became a Christian. He was born in a Buddhist village of about 150 households in Burma, now called Myanmar. There were no schools in the villages in those days, so he went to the Buddhist monastery for education for about ten years.

After this, Tawd went into the Buddhist temple as a novice for five years, and then went on to be a full Buddhist monk for the next 15 years of his life. In order to gain a bachelor's degree in Buddhism, he left his village. As he studied in the Buddhist university, Tawd progressed as high as he could in the Buddhist religion. The Buddhist leaders in the Sangha recognized him as a teaching lecturer in Buddhism. They sent him to visit many cities and towns throughout the land to lecture on Buddhism.

One day he went to teach in a certain town where many of the people spoke English. Since he could not speak English fluently, Tawd decided he would learn English so that he could speak with the people in that area about Buddhism. He found that the only qualified teacher to help him with English was a lay Christian leader who was pastoring a little church in town without pay. His name was Mr. Thom.

In time Tawd approached Thom and asked if he would teach him English. Pastor Thom said he would be glad to do so, but that he had two conditions. First, Tawd would have to meet with him every day for an hour between 8:00 a.m. and 9:00 a.m. This gave the pastor repeated contact with Tawd. Secondly, Thom said they would need a textbook, and the textbook that he chose as the instructor was the New Testament in English. The pastor understood that the Word of God would eventually speak for itself. Tawd accepted these two conditions, saying, "For me no problem." The real reason the Buddhist priest wanted to learn English was to get a wider knowledge by reading English Buddhist books. For six months Tawd studied daily with Thom so he could spread Buddhism among the English speakers there.

After some time, Tawd, the Buddhist priest, came across John 14:6 and seemed to be in confusion over this verse. He asked himself how could this be? The Buddha claimed to "only point the way," but Jesus said, "I am the way." The Buddha said, "The light arose within me," but Jesus declared, "I am the light of the world." The Buddha said, "I learn truth by self-intuition," but Jesus affirmed, "I am the truth, I am the way." So these questions challenged Tawd day and night. The "I ams" of Jesus contrasted with the "I know" of the Buddha. What was the truth about the Truth? Slowly, through the study of the Bible and discussions with the pastor, the light dawned upon Tawd. He became motivated to change and soon accepted Christ. He did leave the priesthood soon after.

Tawd explained to me that the Buddha's philosophy was so rich and full of good teaching, but it questioned God. The Buddhist scholars did not believe in Creator God, so Tawd's dilemma was centered on "no God" versus the God of the Bible. The Buddha himself claimed "omnisense" (self knowing) for himself. As Tawd meditated on the Bible he began to discover God as Creator, Sustainer and Savior. He already felt that merits of humans cannot fulfill the demands of karma. He had faithfully done lots of practice of the 227 rules

35

to follow as a Buddhist priest, but still felt unfulfilled. These were just the basic laws, but actually there are thousands and thousands of rules to follow on the way to "purity." How could he fulfill all of those? It was impossible and hopeless for any person. Tawd concluded that in Buddhism the future was not sure, and that there was not much hope of attaining nirvana either.

In contrast, he told Thom that the Lord Jesus said, "I know you are my witnesses." Here was present assurance and hope. So despite the high Buddhist standards in Tawd's own life, he suddenly realized that hope and true life were to be found only in Christ. In this Savior are all the promises of God. This added double joy. Tawd did not reject the good parts of the teaching of Buddha, but recognized that Buddha had only part of the truth and part of the light, because Buddha himself was searching for truth. He believed that by discovering Christ in relationship to God's revelation, he had found the truth. In Buddhism the merits leading to twenty heavens and the demerits leading to many hells were to be contrasted with God's grace provided in Christ received freely by faith alone. Certainly, karma is a judge, but karma and merit cannot balance each other out, Tawd argued.

Today Tawd is very elderly but still teaching young Christians how to relate to and witness to their Buddhist neighbors, friends and families. Thom has been dead for many years. The grace of God's gospel is still the "power of God unto salvation to everyone who believes" (Romans 1:16).

SECTION TWO

THE GOSPEL FACING BUDDHIST CULTURES

Current statistics clearly indicate that the bulk of non-Christian populations are concentrated in Asia among three large blocks of people—the Chinese, the Hindus, and the Muslims (Winter 1977: 123-126). The Buddhist bloc comes next. In all four of these populations, only comparatively small numbers have responded to the gospel of Christ. It is also unlikely that during the last three decades in China, centuries of Buddhist philosophical thinking would be entirely wiped out. Certainly changes have occurred, but a lot of Buddhist conceptualization mixed with spiritistic beliefs probably still pervades Chinese thinking today. Thus the Buddhist peoples may form the largest group of unreached people today. The Chinese alone claim a population of one billion—a quarter of the world's population and one third of the unevangelized three billion today. It is therefore most fitting that thought be given to presenting the gospel to a Buddhist culture.

Vital Issues

The Christian Church among Buddhist peoples, whether the Mahayana or the Theravada school, is a tiny minority, usually less than 1% of the population with rare exceptions, notably Korea. Consequently the vital theological issues concerning the gospel and the Buddhist culture focuses around at least three major areas, all of which are somewhat inter-related:

1. The survival of the church facing solid social solidarity and opposition.
2. The development of a sense of belonging or identity within the unfavorable context and climate.

3. The need to communicate Christ acceptably to Buddhists so that the church can extend and penetrate the barriers of social resistance.

Two specific areas for study should be identified: 1) Ethnotheology and 2) Evangelistic Theology and Strategy. Both should progress side by side. The church must be kept from becoming an insular sub-society, which fails to communicate Christ effectively to its Buddhist neighbors. Ethnotheology must therefore take into account communicating the gospel to the dominant population in its development. My main emphasis will be on this evangelistic communication.

This book will not deal in depth or detail with the many facets of this vast and complicated subject. It will, however, briefly set the topic in perspective. Essential differences between Buddhism and Christianity are highlighted as well as the problem of the communication of the gospel. The last half of the paper focuses on some strategies and practical approaches for presenting the gospel to Buddhists.

Christian Encounter with Buddhists

In its two thousand five hundred year history, Buddhism has been one of the great religions of the world. The main expansion occurred during the first two millennia. Kenneth S. Latourette observed that its growth among people of high civilizations or advanced religion, did not fully displace its religious predecessors. It was only among peoples "where the prevailing religion was animism, that Buddhism became dominant" (1956:43). Actually even here, it dominated but did not dislodge animism. Buddhism has made no significant advance in the last five centuries, except possibly in the West.

Christian encounter with Buddhists can be traced a long way back to the Nestorian period. Richard Garbe writes, "Christian influence on Buddhism in Tibet and China has been possible since AD635, for from this year we have evidence of a Nestorian mission that set out for those lands under a leader by the name of Olopan or Alopen" (1959:176).

Despite continual Christian encounters since that time, early Roman Catholic missions followed by Protestant ones produced only meager results in terms of church growth. In fact some of the earlier missions to Buddhist peoples in Asia did not even survive. Three main causes account for the lack of permanent self-perpetuating Christian communities among Buddhist peoples. First is persecution, second is syncretism, and third is the failure of the church to break through the social solidarity of Buddhist communities. These still pose basic problems facing Christian theologians and evangelists today.

Recognizing some historical and doctrinal similarities between Christianity and Buddhism, many people think they are both much the same. Similarities of ethical standards such as the Ten Commandments and the Buddhist Sila (prohibitions) and other observations such as those listed by Paul A. Eakin (1956:27-31) appear to add weight to this. A warning is needed, however, regarding the precise meaning and definition of such concepts and principles so compared. Are they truly equivalent or even similar? Not really!

First, Buddha basically taught the ability of self to free oneself from corruption and suffering, to obtain a state of perfect non-existence, without the help of God. Thus in modern terms, the basis of Buddhism is Humanism, that is, man does not have to answer to a higher authority than himself, and man is basically good and can become good by his own efforts. This he can do without any help from God, or any reference to God. Like other human-initiated religions, Buddhism is a projection of human thinking out to the infinite. Christianity, on the other hand, stems from God's self-disclosure to man. This divine revelation climaxed in the incarnation of our Lord Jesus Christ. The gospel is therefore centered in a transcendent God, revealing Himself in terms of man's own culture and language.

Second, Buddhism rejects the concept of a personal God and for that matter, of any spiritual personality, either human or divine. God in the Christian sense is unknown to Buddhists. In place of a personal Creator they hold the error of *karma*—cause and effect—as the exclusive principle to explain the universe. What or who initiated karma is undetermined. In modern times, God has been interpreted in Buddhist religious terminology. Again the danger of definitions and conceptualization is to be carefully discerned. The following indicated subtle syncretism by taking the Christian form of God into Buddhistic writings, while maintaining basic Buddhist meaning.

Bhikkhu Buddhadasa Indapanno, a leading Buddhist scholar, equated God with karma, rejecting personality in favor of "nature" as cause. In terms of comparison, not equivalents, this is reasonably acceptable thinking, though it begs the question of prime initiation. In gospel terms, God is the final point of orientation for all His purposeful relation to the world. In Buddhism the final cause is the principle of karma. Indapanno also equated God as creator with the Buddhist term, *avijja* (1967:66-67). This means lack of knowledge or ignorance, the basic cause of evil. Hence God in Buddhist terms is ignorance, being the power of nature which caused all things to exist, and as such caused suffering. Such an interpretation of God is absolutely unacceptable.

Third, D.T. Niles brilliantly clarifies the basic Buddhist doctrines of *anicca* (impermanence or transitoriness), *anatta* (soullessness or absence of self), and *dukkha* (sorrow, suffering):

> If we do not start with God we shall not end with Him, and when we start with Him we do not end with the doctrines of *anicca*, *anatta* and *dukkha*.

> The existence of God means the existence of an order of life which is eternal—*nicca* (permanence). It means that there is postulated for the soul—*atta*—an identity which is guarded by God's sovereignty, and that sorrow—*dukkha*—is seen to consist, not so much in the transitoriness of things, as in the perverseness of our wills which seeks these things instead of the things which are eternal. The circle of the Christian faith can thus be described as that which starting with God leads man to the realization that God alone affords the most adequate base for a most meaningful explanation of life's most significant facts (1967:27). (Note: In Pali, the prefix "a" negates, meaning "not.")

Buddha saw life was meaningless in itself, and set out to rescue men from this meaninglessness. Jesus saw life could become meaningful in God, and set out to call men to share that meaning (John 10:10). Furthermore, in Buddhism, death is the final category. In the gospel, the final category is life (Niles 1967:29,34,35). Buddhists seek to shorten life, to escape from the never ending cycle of rebirths. The gospel emphasizes everlasting life.

A fourth contrast shows that true Christianity is centered in altruism. Because karma encourages preoccupation with self-dependence, Buddhism becomes self-centered. This social difference is significant. The Buddhist social order is dominated by the individual, and there is a lack of sense of relation, man to man, and man to God

(Eakin 1965:56, 63). In Thailand, for instance, it is almost inconceivable for the Buddhist to believe that the missionary has come out of pure concern for them without an incentive for personal gain. They often ask the question, "What are you getting out of this? A higher salary? Government sponsorship? More merit? Or what?" The concept of selfless constraining love of Christ for others is foreign to Buddhist thinking.

To the Christian the way up is down, taking the servant role, being a doormat to fellow men. To the Buddhist the way up is a self-centered preoccupation. To walk over others or use them for your own advancement is acceptable. Of course it can be noted that in all men, even among Christians, such attitudes can prevail, but they are contrary to the biblical gospel.

Another major difference is in the principle of salvation, or ultimate attainment. For the Buddhist, self-effort and "boot-strap" deliverance through their own human energies and ability, is a cardinal principle. "Depend only on self."

The gospel on the other hand declares that dependence on self and confidence in the flesh spells doom. We are utterly helpless apart from the grace of God in Christ alone. Salvation comes through dependence on Almighty God, made operational through the penitent's faith (Eph. 2:8-9, Gal. 2:20, 3:7, Rom. 3:28, 4:1-28).

Furthermore, Buddhist karma tends to engender fatalism, hopelessness, self-excusing and pessimism in the majority of the population. Buddhism has no possibility of forgiveness, for "Karma is the iron law to which there is no exception"(Appleton 1958:52). Contrast this with the gospel of the loving God who gives forgiveness, hope, and an exchanged life, manifested in a spiritual dimension through the power of Jesus Christ's shed blood. Christ's atonement is sufficient for cleansing from the past, power in the present, and hope in the future.

The honest evangelist or theologian settles for neither integrative syncretism, nor a fully indigenized Buddhistic gospel. Both would distort the true meaning. An expression of the gospel in Buddhistic cultures must be dynamically equivalent to the pristine biblical core and clothed in meaningful communicative garb appropriate to each cultural context.

In this present time when cultural relativism, situational ethics, secularism and humanism are flooding the communicative media, pressures are brought upon the church and her emissaries to reduce the uniqueness of Christ, the authority of the Bible, and the necessity of the Christian gospel, to an "on-par" level with other world religions. Through this the Church is in danger of being swallowed up by a gross life. Unfortunately, sometimes seminaries perpetuate this lie—professors teach it, students believe it. Christians, however, must reject its error. Faithful missionaries, church leaders and Christians everywhere must resist this unscriptural philosophy.

At the same time a call for sympathetic understanding of the Buddhist in his dilemma is needed. A Christian approach should always be with humility and loving persuasion, backed by the testimony of dynamic personal relationship with Jesus Christ. A living demonstration of the gospel, not a pharisaical preciseness of evangelical doctrines, is required. Everywhere men are lost in sin, alienated from God their Creator. An increased concern to communicate the gospel to the Buddhist and renewed zealous evangelism to present Christ the only Savior is urgently needed. The effectiveness of Christ's ambassadors will be proportionate to the dependence on the power of the Holy Spirit and their sensitivity to the cultural concepts of those to whom they go.

Effective Evangelism Demands Effective Communication

The contextual barriers to cross-cultural communication are many, particularly to the Buddhists. The social solidarity of the religious overlay is strong. Thai culture itself is deeply steeped in Buddhism. The religious and educational language is heavily infiltrated with Buddhistic terms, connotations, and concepts. The gospel through its dynamic expansion, the Reformation and evangelical awakenings established a Christian moral base in many Western nations. Buddhism likewise tied together the fragmented peoples of Asia, particularly those animistic populations in the process of culture change and group integration. Thus theology, learned behavior and education at home or school, are saturated with foundational Buddhistic teachings. This religious overlay forms the framework or grid in which communication takes place.

Consider some of the hindrances in this communicational dilemma applicable to the evangelist, theologian or Christian medico-social worker. First, many unwittingly believe that communication is what is said, rather than what is heard. How often we hear, "What a clear presentation of the gospel!" Our main concern should really be, how clear was the reception? In Buddhist lands, the linguistic terms the Christian uses are inevitably loaded with Buddhistic meaning and often are identical in language terms. The preacher or teacher has in mind a Christian concept of sin, heaven, hell, God, faith or whatever, but as he speaks he uses Buddhist words loaded with Buddhistic connotations. Is it any wonder that Buddhists listening to him often reply, "Oh, if that is Christianity, it is just the same as Buddhism."

Second, the frustration of the gospel proclaimer revolves around the problem of meaning. The communicator fails to remember that he cannot transfer meaning. The Christian may encode the message, but the Buddhist must decode it. Therefore the communicator can only transfer "bits" of information. The meaning is then formed in the mind of the receiver in terms of his own cultural grid. This is equally true for the cross-cultural missionary as well as for a Ceylonese Christian speaking to a Buddhist neighbor.

The solution demands action to establish a circle of a communicative process. Communication is not portrayed by a straight line. It is not a verbal echo or rebound of the actual words. Effective communication requires the reflex of the hearer's understanding the meaning, equivalent to that sent by the encoder. Thus a feedback mechanism is essential for evaluating honest communication. Conversational interchange is helpful here, rather than just the "pulpit announcing" mode.

Listening is therefore a vital part of the process of effective communication, especially for audiences such as Buddhists whose comprehension is based on diametrically opposed presuppositions and premises. The more interchange and feedback to clarify meaning occurs, especially through successive repeated contact, the more likely biblical understanding is to be conceived.

Nevertheless, while preciseness of communication is a requirement of theological responsibility, it is the Holy Spirit alone who communicates spiritual truth. There are times when the Holy Spirit works, despite the ignorance and blunders of the preacher. However, this is no excuse for failing to make determined efforts to sharpen clear communication of the gospel.

Local Flavored Media
In Asian cultures, especially among rural and tribal populations, oral communication forms are basic and

tend to predominate. The electronic and print media in such populations usually have a low profile as local communicative media. Studies in ethno-media such as indigenous song, dance, drama, music and other arts are urgently needed in many Buddhist cultures. Research and experimentation with pilot projects should be implemented. Evaluating and measuring the effectiveness of increased communication is needed. Use and adaptation of the grassroots media should be encouraged in all teaching. In urban areas and some rural ones too, some Western forms of media such as films have been somewhat indigenized. Christian communicators should carefully study the indigenized principles and process behind the acceptance of such media, and not glibly follow Western mode and psychology in utilizing these media.

Every Christian should be concerned to find meaningful expressions and indigenous illustrations applicable to communicating theological truth. To use a Buddhist Thai idiom, "108" illustrations from daily life are pregnant with meaning, awaiting spiritual application. The evangelist and theologian should constantly be on the lookout for keen historical illustrations, powerful in the minds of the hearers, to apply spiritual truth through them. For example in Thailand, the theological concept of substitution which presupposes someone vicariously giving his life for another is incongruous with Buddhist religious beliefs. A beautiful historical illustration of the famous Queen Suriyothai of the Ayuthia period helps open the windows of understanding here. Briefly stated, the Thai King went out to fight the opposing Burmese ruler. Suriyothai dressed up disguised as a Thai warrior. Unbeknown to her royal husband, she rode out to the battle. In the ensuing fight the Thai King was losing the advantage. He was about to be cut down. Seeing this, the Queen deliberately drove her elephant between the Burmese King and her husband. She was slain by the long-handled knife wielded by the Burmese ruler, but her husband escaped. He later built a special memorial to her in honor of her bravery and sacrifice. The gospel application is obvious.

The use of parable, symbol and analogy is generally more acceptable to the Buddhist mind than strictly focused arguments. Word pictures can be employed to advantage. The Bible is full of rich parables and illustrations. However, missionaries and Christians tend to over-explain these instead of letting the meaning shine forth. Parables or analogy are great ways to get the Buddhist to open up for discussion, thereby helping him evaluate the gospel's meaning. To large sections of Buddhist populations, the majority of whom are rural, Pauline arguments in strict linear logic form, such as those in the book of Romans, are difficult to follow. Their minds tend to be conditioned more to contextual type logic, similar to the spokes in a wheel pointing to a common hub of meaning. Such an approach is used in Hebrews. Studying the indigenous process of communication and utilizing these principles for proclamation and teaching will probably be a crucial issue in effective evangelism and theological education. This is true both for national church leaders and foreign apostles.

Some Theological Strategies and Approaches

Many approaches have been suggested and tried in presenting the gospel to Buddhists. No major breakthrough has been seen through the use of any one method, strategy or approach. This is not surprising as it is a much better principle to tailor the approach to the individual or particular group being reached. Buddhist beliefs vary dramatically even within one country, as do the people groups (homogeneous units). Therefore the Christian evangelist and theologian must be sensitive to take this into consideration. Several approaches will be suggested.

1) The Apologetic Approach. First is the apologetic approach to the thinking Buddhist. Some Christian theologians feel there are many contrasts between Buddhism and Christianity, which are in fact largely opposites in concept. Inconsistencies in Buddhism then form the basis of argument to logically convince Buddhists of the gospel. Dorothy Beugler concisely listed some of these contrasts and inconsistencies in *The Religion of the Thai in Central Thailand*.

Paul A. Eakin suggests the most effective presentation of Christ will be made by those who know and sympathetically study Buddhism, rather than the Christian who is ignorant of it. He feels, however, that the gospel should be presented to the Buddhist mind with the "explosive force of a brand new affection." He affirms also that the Buddhist will not reach Christ better or clearer through the medium of Buddhist philosophy. His apologetic centers around two main "gaps." First a challenge to the traditional Buddhist cosmology, using Genesis to convince the truth of God as Creator of the world and men. The second focal point of Eakin's approach is the fact of salvation, and the possibility of forgiveness and remission of penalty through Christ (1956:61-62).

Significantly, Daniel McGilvary, pioneer apostle to northern Thailand, gained his first convert, Nan Inta, by predicting the total eclipse of the sun on August 17, 1868. Nan Inta, a Buddhist abbot and diligent student of Buddhism, had argued with McGilvary on subjects such as the science of geography, the shape of the earth, the nature of eclipses, and so on. Of course there is much myth in unfounded scientific concepts in early

Buddhist cosmology. Finally, when Nan Inta saw the eclipse as predicted, his faith in the old cosmology was shattered. He turned and became a Christian. He was one of thousands to turn to Christ in north Thailand in the next half century (McGilvary 1912:96-97).

Wan Petchsongkram also likes the apologetic method, and centers his arguments around the person of God and God as Creator (1975:54f, 64f). He also deals with such conflicting interpretations or concepts within Buddhism as *vinyaan* (soul, spirit) and *nipaan* (nirvana) (1975:39f, 119f).

Preaching about God must be done so as not to make God seem evil in terms of Buddhist thinking. A new interpretation of *avijja* must be taught starting not with God the Creator (Genesis 1, 2) but with the Fall of Man (Genesis 3) as the real source of ignorance and consequent suffering.

Another leading elderly Thai apologist, Boonmi Rungruangwongs, argued bluntly in his Thai booklets on "God," "Desire," and a 22-point rationale for killing animals. He does this, however, in the context of Buddhist thought.

One of the best published approaches presenting the gospel to the Buddhist is *Buddhism and the Claims of Christ* by D.T. Niles (1967). It is written in a style compatible with the thought patterns of the Buddhist mind, yet from a thoroughly Christian viewpoint. I recommend it.

I have found that the apologetic approach has been valuable in teaching Christians to understand their faith in contrast to the Buddhist way, rather than as a prime strategy for winning groups of Buddhists to Christ. Most of those who take the apologetic approach usually claim their approach is to the thinking, educated Buddhist. However, most Buddhists do not fall into this category.

2) **The "Point of Contact" Approach.** A second approach is through the use of Buddhism as a stepping stone to Christianity. Ethical and moral similarities are used as the basis for presenting Christ. Some look at the doctrine of karma as dealing with an incompleteness, rather than an absolute falsehood—an incompleteness which is to find its fulfillment in Christ. In seeking what Don Richardson calls "redemptive analogies" in Buddhism, one becomes quite frustrated. However, in the animistic foundations of many Buddhist societies, careful research may identify some redemptive analogies. God is the God of all cultures. He has allowed certain elements to be placed within different cultures to be used as bridges for the gospel. For example, among animistic beliefs, the Sawi Tribe in Indonesian West Irian had a custom of offering a peace child in order to bring about and restore normal relations between warring villages. The application to God's Peace Child resulted in the establishment of a church among the Sawi. Similarly, the Yali people had a practice of assigned places of refuge, a beautiful transition to Numbers 35 and the Place of Refuge in Christ. Another tribe has an impressive and symbolic ceremony of the new birth. Sometimes elements such as these have been left within cultures as residual reference back to the original creation and fall of man and to the true redemptive plan of God. They lay latent waiting for Christian emissaries to apply them as levers or springboards for preaching and teaching the gospel.

Three times I have visited Korea, a Buddhist land where a strong Christian movement has taken place since 1907. One key to Korean church growth under the Holy Spirit was a missionary's choice of an indigenous name for God: "Hananim." Once a year the Korean King would go to an island in the middle of the river within the capital to make special offerings to

"Hanylnim" who was thought of as a high lofty being in heaven, i.e. Hanyl. When early missionaries taught about Hanylnim in deeper terms, with a more intimate and authoritative knowledge of him than the Korean King or elders had, the people listened. This was a significant element in turning thousands of Koreans to Christ. Soon "Hananim" (Hana = one), a more biblically accurate term, became widely accepted among Protestants.

One particular Buddhist point of contact that some missionaries have used should be noted. As mentioned earlier, a movement among northern Thai Buddhists occurred between 1884 and 1914 in the days of Daniel McGilvary. Between these years the church grew from 152 members to 6,900. Usually such growth is caused by a number of intertwining causes. One of these elements, however, appears to have come from a Buddhist point of contact. In 1895 W. Clifton Dodd wrote a brief article "Siam and the Laos" in which he noted "the providential preparation" of the northern Thai Buddhists for the gospel. He referred to "the preparation of Buddhism" whose "meaningless ritual in an unknown tongue (the Pali)" provided "inadequate answers for either head or heart" (1895:8-10). Dodd, a veteran missionary to the Lao, as the ethnic northern Thai were then known, suggested that "the more positive preparations are found in the Laos Buddhist books" as against the negative failure to keep the people from worshipping the spirits. Indeed one of the factors which had some bearing on this movement was the Buddhist teaching of a future savior. At least three names referred to this final savior: 1) Phra See An, 2) Phra Ahreyah Metrai (also spelled Maitreya), and 3) Phra Pho Thi Sat. (This last one is also known to Chinese Buddhists.) Part of this Buddhist mythical prophecy says:

Myriads of ages ago a white crow laid five eggs; that each of these eggs was to hatch and bring forth a Buddha; that these Buddhas were to appear in the upper world, one by one; that four have already appeared; and that *the last is about to come.* The people believed that *he will be the greatest and best of all*; that he will gloriously reign 84,000 years, and that in his time, all men will become pure in heart (Harris 1906:214, italics mine).

Dodd also wrote of a widely prevalent tradition concerning Punyah Tum, a kind of John the Baptist:

Its advent is to be heralded by a forerunner, Punyah Tum, who will prepare the way; the rough placed shall be made as smooth as "Temple ground". Then the elder brother of Buddha is to become incarnate as a savior. His name is Alen-Yah Metrai (sic). Only the good shall be able to see him, but all who see him shall be saved. The proclamation to the Laos people of this fullness of time and the completed salvation is predicted to be by a foreigner from the South. He is to be a man with white hair and a long beard, who will not fly in the air like a bird, neither will he walk on the earth like a beast, but who will come bringing in his hands the true ten commandments (Beach 1902:315).

The impact of pioneer Daniel McGilvary's appearance in the North in the light of this expectation must have impressed many of the Christians. A witness to the arrival of McGilvary on one of his northern tours, described him as "a man with long, white beard, mounted on an elephant. When he dismounted he began teaching out of a book" (McFarland 1928:183).

Arthur J. Brown quoted Dodd and Briggs in relation to "a general expectation of another reincarnation of

Buddha" (1908:343). Dodd said:

Most of our auditors looked upon Jesus as the next Buddha, the Savior, Ahreyah Metrai. Many lifted both hands in worship of the pictures, the books, and the preachers. Our colporteurs were treated in most places as the messengers of the Buddhist Messiah. Offerings of food, flowers, and wax tapers were made to them. In return, they were expected to bless the rivers. They explained that they themselves were sinners deriving all merits and blessing from God, and then reverently asked a blessing from Him. Thus Christian services were held in hundreds of homes.

Dr. Briggs reported of one of his tours:

The message was received with outspoken gratitude and intelligent interest, many of the people remaining long after midnight, reading the books and tracts by the light of the fire and asking questions of the Christians in our company. These people, hungry for truth that satisfies and longing for light, are very anxiously awaiting the coming of the promised Messiah of Buddhism.

Some of the missionaries capitalized on these predictions "pointing to the salvation wrought out by the blessed Son of God." They used this as a starting point of contact within the Buddhist culture to bridge the religio-cultural gap in meaningful communication. They went on to expound the riches of Christ.

Most missionaries, however, were cautious in using this Buddhistic lever as an approach. Many of the finer details were contrary to the biblical account. There was no complete comparison of Ahreyah Metrai and Christ, nor did they attempt to integrate or synthesize the two. It was only a point of contact, an interest awakener.

Christian missionaries avoided giving credence and authority to Buddhist writings. They maintained a high view of the authority and uniqueness of the biblical revelation. They were also careful not to syncretize Christ into the Buddhist structure; they preached a unique Savior, the Lord Jesus Christ, in their evangelism.

This illustration may be irrelevant to modern Buddhists today. Nevertheless the sensitive search for adequate points of contact should continue. Meaningful bridges to the people should be explored.

3) The Shame Theology Approach. A third approach focuses on a theological difference between Shame and Guilt. Among the "losing face" societies of Buddhist Asia, shame rather than guilt is a dominant trait in culture. Theologically speaking, there is considerable room for investigating this theme in relation to the gospel's approach to the Buddhist. Lowell L. Nobel has made a worthy contribution here in his anthropological, biblical and sociological study of shame, entitled *Naked and Not Ashamed.* He makes some interesting observations on this subject related to Japan, China and Thailand (1957:46-63). Joseph R. Cook's paper "The Gospel for Thai Ears" also majors on the "shame" approach.

Thus the evangelistic message becomes "sin-shame-Savior" in place of "sin-guilt-Savior." Actually shame is referred to in Scripture more than guilt. More research and study should be done on the shame approach. A number of problems still need to be clarified. One of the main issues is overcoming the Buddhistic preoccupation with self and an acceptance of accountability to God. Western and national theologians must think this approach through in terms of the conceptual definitions of Buddhistic cultures. Shame in the West is not necessarily identical to shame in the East.

In a "losing face" or shame culture, one can have

shame from purely selfish reasons alone, especially in Thailand's individualistic society. The theological issue is to see in one's shame a responsibility to others and especially to God. The shame approach, to have biblical basis, must overcome the syndrome of purely revolving around self. There are points where shame does have a wider orientation.

4) The "Scratch Where It Itches" Approach. Fourth is a "scratch where it itches" theology. Christ always applied His message to the appropriate needs of the individual or group. He was constantly teaching to their need, applying the gospel where the people hurt. Christianity needs to be practical in these days, not just in the demonstration of good works, but also in applying their teachings to the real needs of the people. Evangelists and theologians should observe carefully and listen conscientiously to the heartbeat of the community. Research and surveys are needed to discover the deep-felt needs of various people groups. We must find out where people are itching and then scratch there with the gospel. Theologizing divorced from the real needs of people is futile. But so is social service without gospel pronouncement.

Furthermore, through this incarnational approach to the community, the gospel minister builds his credibility among the people. He sits where they sit and feels as they feel. He also becomes a living demonstration of the gospel he proclaims, as he ministers and teaches to those needs.

Patience is needed when working with Buddhist people. A time for *diffusion* of the message is usually necessary. Gospel saturation helps break the ignorance barriers over a period of time. Few people in Asia know much about the true gospel, yet the evangelist often expects them to make an immediate decision for Christ.

Rather he should evaluate where each community is on the "scale of awareness" devised by Engel and Norton (1975:45). He can then decide what would be the next most appropriate action to take in leading them towards Christ.

Also one aim should be to locate the receptive families and responsive units of the population. These should be the prime focus for intensive evangelism and teaching. No amount of impersonal approach from a high pulpit will effectively do this. As personal contact at the grassroots defines the needs and hopes of people, then the balm of the gospel can be applied. As H. Richard Niebuhr concluded in his book *Christ and Culture* (1956), "Christ is the transformer of culture."

In the midst of cultural change, innovation and acculturation, the sociological factors of communities must be taken into consideration in our preaching and our theological approaches. Urban populations today may not be so much Buddhist as secularist and materialist. Nevertheless, the underlying Buddhist assumptions will be similar.

A beautiful illustration of "scratching where it itches" is seen in the Thailand Southern Baptists' approach to the slums. A whole strategy based on sociological surveys of need and practical Christian involvement is helping meet those needs along with the teaching and preaching of the gospel. Their objective is to establish local house churches grounded in the local community.

It is significant to observe that much church growth in Buddhist lands has been initiated at the point of human weakness. Man's extremity has become God's opportunity for church growth. Henry Otis Dwight, referring to the large blocs of non-Christian populations under Buddhism, Islam and such, says that these "bulwarks of resistance" loom large before the church as "great hostile fortresses all long the line of her advance." Dwight suggests looking for cracks in the resistant walls, or flaws in the stubborn strongholds as "strategic points for effective evangelism." Thus by locating smaller units of responsiveness, often inconspicuous among the dominant population, missionaries avoid "striking in force at a main center before its time has come" (1905:82-83). Of course the large resistant blocks must not be neglected. Research and various approaches to them must be found. But in the meantime those cracks and flaws must be utilized to the full. The opportunities must be taken. Ripening fields must be harvested.

Many Buddhists who have come to Christ have first come "to the end of themselves." Many conversions from Buddhism swing on the pivot point of the inability to accomplish perfection by oneself.

In rural Thailand the movement amongst leprosy patients is an example. They found their social, physical, and spiritual needs met through missionary leprosy clinics and subsequently Christian churches. I have described some of that process in the book *Strategy to Multiply Rural Churches* (1977:134-135). Numerous other people have also turned to Christ because of other medical extremities and their contact with Christians in clinics or hospitals (Smith 1977:173).

Another point of weakness is the pressure from evil spirit oppression or witchcraft. Many of those who turned from Buddhism to Christ in the early movement in north Thailand did so to obtain freedom from witchcraft accusations and the social ostracism associated with it. I have met quite a few cases of Buddhists who became Christians to be freed from spirit oppression or possession. They had prayed to Buddha and other gods, made offerings to the spirits, worshiped idols, gone into the priesthood, and still had no release. Frustrated, they met Jesus at the point of their extremity (Smith 1977:158).

Others come to Christ out of economic extremity or impoverishment. Disaster, flood or famine have met up with them. Their karma has overplayed itself. They are fed up, hopeless, frustrated and discouraged. Hearing the gospel and seeing Christ's love through His servants often turns some to Christ.

Another pointed case is the Southeast Asian refugees from Buddhist lands, now over 100,000 in Thailand alone. These were a very receptive people especially in the early days of their freedom. At the point of their exasperation and frustration they sought for someone to truly depend on. Is it any wonder that the Thailand Southern Baptists alone baptized 2,100 Cambodian and Vietnamese refugees during the three years following 1975?

In all these cases, motivation may differ from person to person. The exact motivation for turning people to Christianity at the point of their extremity is not always clear. Nevertheless, this opportunity to teach, preach and nurture these people in the ways of God's Word provides an approach to Buddhist people that must never be neglected.

In recent decades most of the major Buddhist lands in Asia today have been through some traumatic experience. Political and military excursions, and in some cases complete takeovers, have challenged the very core of these countries and their religion. In the trauma of today when national crises, economic chaos and military clashes are prevalent in Asia, one wonders, "Is God bringing the Buddhist nations to an extremity, to an end of trusting in themselves, in order to steer them towards the gospel of His grace, and to cause them to call out in utter dependence on the One who alone can help?"

Another clue to the frustrations of many relates to the question of death. Many Buddhists fear hell, death, and the afterlife. There is deep concern for all the ancestral spirits and the retribution that will come to those who fail to give obeisance to them. Further research is needed to find out at what point the gospel truly "clicks" with those deep-seated fears and aspirations of the Buddhist heart's need.

5) The Power Encounter Approach. Finally, since Buddhist nations have a more modified animism than pure Buddhism, we must accept the possibility that the power encounter element is a most strategic approach. A leading Buddhist scholar writes that from the long distant past "Thai Buddhists have had a god." This is clearly shown in the word *phrachao,* a truly Thai term referring to "something which one fears and must beseech or flatter, an instinct among all thinking beings." Even before Brahmanism or Buddhism came, the Thai people believed in some kind of god in terms of spirit and divine being. The Brahmans introduced the concept of the King as an incarnation of god, hence the original word *phrachao* was also used for the King. The personal term "I" then became *Khaphrachao.* (*Kha* means servant-slave and *chao* or *phrachao* means lord or god.) When Buddhism became dominant, there was a tendency to glorify each king as a Buddha. The first-person pronoun was then changed to *Khaphra-Buddhachao,* which in its present day use has been abbreviated to *Khapachao* (Indapanno 1967:61,63).

Furthermore, Thai Buddhists have a deep respect for *phra,* an impersonal quantitative supernatural power. Many other beliefs and concepts involve power in holy water, incantations, tattoos, amulets, and miniature phra objects they hang around their necks or other parts of the body (*khryang raang khong khlang*). Most of these are tied up with the concern for protection, security and invulnerability, or for power over others especially in economic and love life.

Thus the gospel should present Christ as the superior power over all these elements. Using this *power approach* I noticed increased response in Thailand. The message of power might be presented as follows:

1. God is the original source of all power and perfection. The Lord Jesus Christ is the all-powerful Lord. He is Creator and Governor over all. (John 1:1-3, Colossians 1:16-17)

2. God created man in the image of God, and gave him power to govern the world. Man was originally perfect and enjoyed his freedom and power in the presence of God without shame, sin or death. (Gen. 1:26-27, 2:7-25)

3. Man lost that power through his own willful disobedience and rebellion against God. He then came under the power of evil and demonic spirits, resulting in suffering, shame and death. Man thus started the process of "karma" and became slave to sin. (Gen. 3, Rom. 5:12, John 8:34, Eph. 2:1-3)

4. The Lord Jesus Christ saw man had no possible way to free himself from the power of Satan, sin, and karma. Christ came down to break the power of Satan in man's life, to set him free from the power of evil spirits, and to redeem him from sin and karma. By the miracle of dying in man's place, He bore the penalty of man's sin and shame. The perfect sinless Jesus restores God's power in man's life and gives him a new quality of life connected spiritually to God Himself. (John 1:14, 18, 29)

5. Man can have this power through repentance and faith by receiving Christ as his Lord and Source of constant dependence. God, through His grace, gives this power freely, apart from man's work or merit. God gives this power to man through His Holy Spirit whom His disciples are to obey. (John 1:10-13,

15:26, 16:12-15)

6. Christians must share this gospel of power and freedom from karma with their relatives, friends, neighbors and nation. (Acts 1:8, Ezek. 3:19-20)

Obviously a polemical foundation teaching the existence of God is vital. The power encounter approach still requires time for diffusion, teaching and saturation. A group movement usually arises from an inside innovator or prophet who takes God at His word. His bold demonstration of breaking with the old way is often the spark that ignites a greater movement.

The Bible abounds with illustrations of power encounter—the challenge of the power of God applied against the power of evil, Satan, and the demonic world. For example, Gideon destroying the family spirit grove; Elijah challenging the population and priests at Mount Carmel; Daniel's three friends in the fiery furnace; and Daniel proving the power of God in the lions' den. Truly the superiority of the power of Christ above everything else in our lives is the only dynamic approach that will bring Buddhists to a living relationship with Christ. The challenge of Joshua was a power encounter call: "Choose ye this day whom ye will serve — Jehovah or those other gods? But as for me and my house, we will serve the Lord" (Joshua 24:14-15). The social solidarity of the family in this call is applicable to Buddhist lands today. Herein the church will grow and receive its stability and permanence in the midst of a socially antagonistic society.

Conclusion

The practical conclusion in terms of reality of the task before us calls for a theology dealing with three basic issues. First the spiritual conflict demands concentrated prayer to break the controlling forces of darkness in the heavenlies. God has and will answer prayer, but the demonic forces may hinder and frustrate His answers being appropriated at times (Dan. 9:3-4, 17-23). Ask God to break down these powers and to free Buddhist hearts to hear the Word of God through the Holy Spirit.

Second is the socio-cultural clash. This solid social coherence comes largely from the religious thinking. To be Thai in most people's mind means to be Buddhist. To turn from being a Buddhist is like becoming a traitor to one's own nation. What widespread conditions will prepare the Buddhist population for social change in religion? There are signs of such changes at work today.

Third is the bold, though humble, confrontation of the gospel with Buddhism. A dynamic encounter of the living Lord in contrast to the sleeping Buddha is needed. Let those prophetic advocates arise, like Elijah, to demonstrate power encounters. Many lessons are to be learned. More will be gained through sympathetic appreciation of the people than by cold logic. A cultural sensitivity should be welded to incarnational evangelism based on a deep biblical foundation. This requires a person-centered approach while maintaining a truth-centered gospel. To find the best evangelistic approaches to each Buddhist population, much research and careful experimentation should be implemented speedily.

All this calls today's theologians to a new practical task of dealing with various grassroots issues in communication so that large pockets of Buddhist population can and will be won to Jesus Christ, and become functional members in His Church now and in the decades ahead.

Bibliography

Appleton, George. *The Christian Approach to the Buddhist*. London: Edinburgh House Press, 1958.

Beach, Harlan D. *A Geography and Atlas of Protestant*

Missions. New York: Student Volunteer Movement for Foreign Missions, 1901.

Beugler, Dorothy. "The Religion of the Thai in Central Thailand." Mimeographed, undated.

Brown, Arthur J. Article in *Missionary Review of the World*, 1908.

Chaiwan, Saad. *The Christian Approach to Buddhists in Thailand*. Bangkok: Suriyaban Publishers, 1975.

Cooke, Joseph R. "The Gospel for Thai Ears." Mimeographed, unpublished, 1978.

Dodd, W.C. "Siam and the Laos," *Missionary Review of the World*, 1895.

Dwight, Henry Otis (ed). *The Blue Book of Missions for 1905*. New York: Fung & Wagnalls Co., 1905.

Eakin, Paul A. *Buddhism and the Christian Approach to Buddhists in Thailand*. Bangkok: R. Hongladaromp Printer & Publisher, 1956.

Engel, James, and Norton, H. Wilbert. *What's Gone Wrong with the Harvest?* Grand Rapids: Zondervan, 1975.

Garbe, R. *India and Christendom*. Illinois: The Open Court Publishing Co., 1959.

Harris, W. "Unprecedented Opportunity in the Far East," *Students and the Modern Missionary Crusade*. New York: Student Volunteer Movement for Foreign Missions, 1906.

Indapanno, Bhikkhu Buddhadasa. *Christianity and Buddhism*. Bangkok, Sinclaire Thompson Memorial Lectures, fifth series, 1967.

Kaufman, Howard Keva. *Bangkuad: A Community Study in Thailand*. New York: J.J. Augustine, Inc. Publishers, 1960.

Latourette, Kenneth Scott. *Introducing Buddhism*. New

York: Friendship Press, 1958.

McFarland, George Bradley. *Historical Sketch of Protestant Missions in Siam, 1828-1928*. Bangkok: The Bangkok Times Press, Ltd. 1928.

McGilvary, Daniel. *A Half Century Among the Siamese and the Lao*. New York: Fleming H. Revell Co., 1912.

Mole, Robert L. *Thai Values and Behavior Patterns*. Tokyo: Charles E. Tuttle Co., Inc. 1973.

Niebuhr, H. Richard. *Christ and Culture*. New York: Harper & Brothers Publishers, 1956.

Niles, D.T. *Buddhism and the Claims of Christ*. Richmond, Virginia: John Knox Press, 1967.

Noble, Lowell L. *Naked and Not Ashamed*. Michigan: Jackson Printing, 1975.

Petchsongkram, Wan. *Talk in the Shade of the Bo Tree*, translated and edited by Frances E. Hudgins. Bangkok: private printing, 1975.

Pfanner, David E. and Ingersoll, Jasper. "Theravada Thai Comparison," *The Journal of Asian Studies*, Vol. XXI, No. 3, May, 1962.

Smith, Alex G. *Strategy o Multiply Rural Churches (A Central Thailand Case Study)*. Bangkok: OMF Publishers, 1977.

Tambiah, S. *Buddhism and the Spirit Cults in Northeast Thailand*. Cambridge, England: University Press, 1970.

Winter, Ralph D. "Who are the Three Billion?" *Church Growth Bulletin*, Vol. XIII, No. 5, May, 1977.

Originally read and presented as a paper in November 1978 at the Asian Theological Association Annual Meeting held at the University of Singapore. Subsequently published by ATA in 1980 as part of the Asian Perspectives Series.